I0394995

Created and published by Knock Knock
1635-B Electric Avenue
Venice, CA 90291
knockknockstuff.com

Illustrations by Gemma Correll

ISBN: 978-160106783-8
UPC: 825703-50083-7

10 9 8 7 6 5 4 3

Bryce,

100 Reasons to Panic about Being a Grownup

KNOCK KNOCK®
VENICE, CALIFORNIA

Love

Mom

Dec. 2015

1.

You'll have to move out of your parents' basement.*

*You'll no longer be living in your parents' basement.

2.

You're supposed to "do what you love," but that doesn't pay the bills.*

3.

No one wears sweatpants in the real world.*

4.

One word:
Mondays.*

5.

Mom and Dad will take back their emergency credit card.*

*You'll finally learn the value of a hard-earned dollar.

6.

Job interviews are terrifying.*

*They're also ripe with possibility.

7.

Career-wise, you'll start at the bottom.*

8.

You'll lose your youthful spirit.*

*But you'll be able to apply for a mortgage.

Really, you just want to travel and see the world.*

*And . . . what's the problem?

10.

An upgrade from paper plates and plastic sporks will be necessary.*

*You'll be adding less to landfills.

11.

The thought of staying out past your bedtime isn't so attractive anymore.*

*You won't be giving your snooze button a workout.

12.

To afford a place, you'll need to get a roommate.*

*You can also get a cat!

13.

Power suits will become your uniform.*

14.

If you're late, no one will write you a note.*

15.

If you're sick, no one will take care of you.*

*You can cough, sneeze, and wheeze in private.

16.

Your parents will stop treating you to dinner.*

*Finally, you can treat them.
Bonus: you get to choose the restaurant.

17.

It's too late to be a prodigy.*

*You can wait until you're really old;
then you'll be a late bloomer.

18.

You'll be "responsible."*

*And probably suffer fewer hangovers.

19.

Your laundry pile will become a mountain.*

*Think of how accomplished you'll feel after you conquer it!

20.

Making doctor's appointments no longer comes with a parental reminder.*

*Well, there's a use for that calendar sitting on your desk.

21.

You should probably retire your fake ID.*

*You'll only need to keep track of your real name and actual birthday.

22.

Your boss will hate you.*

*Sucking up will be pointless—how freeing!

23.

Making sense
of your money
requires balancing
your checkbook.*

24.

Perusing job listings is depressing.*

*That melancholy could inspire your Steinbeck-esque novel.

25.

You'll compare yourself to other people.*

BOILING
WATER
for
dummies

26.

You'll need to figure out how to boil water.*

*You'll be able to feed yourself.

27.

Filing taxes is a pain.*

*You can finally tackle that pile of receipts
under your bed.

28.

You have no idea
what you're doing
with your life.*

29.

Official documents now require your signature— and your legal responsibility.*

*All that time you spent practicing your John Hancock will finally pay off.

30.

It's official: you've joined the voting public.*

31.

It's time for a budget.*

*You can stop paying for groceries in pennies.

32.

You'll feel lost.*

*You're on a journey—
getting lost is part of the fun.

33.

Going to cool clubs will seem less and less appealing.*

34.

Your bed's not going to make itself.*

*You'll never suffer the indignity of a messy bedroom again.

35.

Getting up before noon is now part of your routine.*

36.

work means deadlines.*

*At least you won't pull all-nighters to
study for tests.

37.

You'll feel compelled to eat healthy stuff— like kale.*

38.

You'll need to start networking.*

39.

who's in charge of car maintenance? You.*

*But you also get to pick what music to play, what bumper stickers to add, and what color fuzzy dice to hang from the rearview mirror.

You'll move to the 'burbs.*

*Well, the schools are better out there.

41.

You'll clip coupons.*

*Hey, you've gotta save for retirement somehow.

42.

Couch-surfing will lose its allure.*

*You might not realize it now, but your back will thank you someday.

43.

You'll wear
sensible shoes.*

*You'll love the arch support.

44.

Your mind will start to go.*

*There's a reason people do crossword puzzles.

45.

Separating your lights and darks is tedious.*

*Your whites will finally stay white.

46.

When younger
people say
"ma'am" or "sir,"
they'll mean you.*

47.

You'll have to remember to take your vitamins.*

GROW UP
Already!
VITAMINS
BORING
FLAVOR

*You won't suffer from malnutrition.

48.

Life will get monotonous.*

49.

Making major decisions is hard!*

50.

You'll stop expressing yourself with wild hair colors.*

*Upkeep will be so much easier.

51.

People will expect
you to know
what's going on in
the world.*

*With a little practice, you'll dazzle them with
your *au courant* small talk.

52.

You'll have to cover up your tattoos.*

*They'll be your inky little secret.

53.

How are you supposed to respond to "so, what do you do?"*

54.

Getting health insurance means figuring out the difference between an HMO and a PPO.*

*You won't have to rely on a homemade splint if you break a bone.

55.

You'll grow apart from your friends.*

56.

You're a night owl—how will you get on a schedule?*

*You can always work the graveyard shift!

57.

You'll have to find a place to live.*

Your new furniture will require assembly.*

*You'll get really good at using an Allen wrench.

59.

You won't know the latest bands— or anything else.*

*You'll have less to worry about.

60.

If you behave badly, your age won't be a good excuse.*

*You can chalk it up to your strong personality.

61.

Your parents are getting older, too.*

*You'll have something in common.

62.

Birthdays will stop being such a big deal.*

Learning to detach from material things is liberating!

63.

Your job will be boring.

*What else do people complain about
at the bar?

64.

Your job will
be stressful.

65.

You'll have to do jury duty.*

*You'll get time off work.

*You'll get time off work.

66.

Trying to get a job means writing cover letters.*

*It's like being your own cheerleader.

67.

Your slang will start to sound dated.*

*You can bring back your favorites.

68.

Your metabolism will slow.*

*You probably needed to cut down
on the cheese puffs anyway.

69.

You'll get a gray hair—or two.*

*It'll make you look distinguished.

70.

You're no longer sheltered from reality.*

71.

You'll have to buy holiday presents instead of just receiving them.*

*Now's the time to learn to make soap, granola, or candles!

72.

You still have to show up for work even when you don't want to.*

73.

If you're into something that the kids are into, you'll just seem creepy.*

*Or extremely cool.

74.

You'll need to learn to cook.*

*You'll get to buy whatever you want
at the grocery store.

75.

People won't take you seriously.*

*You can stop trying so hard.

76.

You'll have a quarter-life crisis.*

*Wouldn't you rather get it over with now
than later?

77.

You'll be pressured to go to lunch with coworkers.*

*You'll get caught up on the hot office gossip.

78.

You won't get invited to go to lunch with coworkers.*

*You'll get caught up on the classics.

79.

You can't nap in the middle of the day.*

*Well, you can, but it's called your lunch hour, and you don't want to return to your cubicle with bedhead, do you?

80.

Phone bills, car
repairs, insurance:
you're paying
your own way
now, baby.*

*With (literal) power comes great responsibility.

81.

You'll go out less.*

*You'll save so much money.

82.

People will start
asking you when
you're going to
get married.*

*At least they're not asking you about kids. Yet.

83.

Your friends will start settling down.*

*Hooray, less competition for suitable mates!

84.

You graduated—with a pile of debt.*

*You got an education out of the deal.

85.

Your job will be soul-sucking.*

*You can devote your spare time to more creative pursuits.

86.

Looking presentable is time-consuming.*

*You'll have an excuse to buy new clothes.

87.

You'll wonder "IS this too young for me?" about certain outfits.*

88.

People will think you're much younger than you are.*

*You can keep getting kids' meals.

89.

People will think you're much older than you are.*

*You'll never get carded.

90.

Teenagers will think you're old.*

91.

You could turn into "the Man."*

92.

Your parents won't invite you on that cruise to Hawaii.*

*They won't force you to pose for cheesy photos.

93.

Maybe you should've gone a little crazier.*

94.

OK, maybe you went a little too crazy.*

*Your grandkids will love your stories.

95.

No one will care when (or if) you get home.*

*No curfew!

96.

You'll go corporate.*

97.

You're getting too old to be a wunderkind.*

98.

No more
summers off.*

*But you won't have to write
papers or study, either.

99.

Your best days are behind you.*

*Or the best is yet to come.

100.

You don't want to grow up.*

*Join the club.

Don't worry. You're in charge now!